Eli Manning

By Jim Gigliotti

Consultant: Craig Ellenport
Former Senior Editor
NFL.com

New York, New York

Credits

Cover, © AP Photo/Bill Kostroun and AP Photo/Bebeto Mathews; Title Page, © Jerry Coli/
Dreamstime; 4, © Roy Dabner/EPA/Newscom; 5, © Mark Cornelison/MCT/Newscom; 6, © Roy
Dabner/EPA/Newscom; 7, © Mark Cornelison/MCT/Newscom; 8, © Jerry Coli/Dreamstime;
9, © Frances M. Roberts/Newscom; 10, © AP Photo/David Rae Morris; 11, © Matt May/ICON SMI/
Newscom; 12, © AP Photo/Chuck Burton; 13, © Bob Leverone/Sporting News/Icon/Newscom;
15, © Joe Robbins; 16, © Imagist/Shutterstock; 17, © AP Photo/Cheryl Gerber; 18, © SBukley/
Dreamstime; 19, © AP Photo/Evan Pincus; 20, Courtesy Guiding Eyes; 21, © Jennifer Mitchell/
Splash News/Newscom; 22, © Jerry Coli/Dreamstime.

Publisher: Kenn Goin
Senior Editor: Joyce Tavolacci
Creative Director: Spencer Brinker
Production and Photo Research: Shoreline Publishing Group LLC
Series Design: Dawn Beard Creative

Library of Congress Cataloging-in-Publication Data

Names: Gigliotti, Jim.
Title: Eli Manning / by Jim Gigliotti.
Description: New York, New York : Bearport Publishing, [2016] | Series:
    Football heroes making a difference | Includes bibliographical references
    and index.
Identifiers: LCCN 2015033442 | ISBN 9781943553402 (library binding) | ISBN
    1943553408 (library binding)
Subjects: LCSH: Manning, Eli, 1981-—Juvenile literature. | Football
    players—United States—Biography—Juvenile literature. | Quarterbacks
    (Football)—United States—Biography—Juvenile literature. | Football
    players—United States—Conduct of life—Juvenile literature.
Classification: LCC GV939.M2887 G54 2016 | DDC 796.332092—dc23
LC record available at http://lccn.loc.gov/2015033442

For more information, write to Bearport Publishing Company, Inc., 45 West 21st Street, Suite 3B,
New York, New York 10010. Printed in the United States of America.

10 9 8 7 6 5 4 3 2 1

CONTENTS

A Dream Come True

Every **NFL** quarterback dreams of the situation Eli Manning found himself in on February 3, 2008. It was Super Bowl XLII (42), and Eli and his New York Giants teammates were battling the New England Patriots. New England led 14–10 in the final minute of the game. The Giants had the ball at the Patriots' 13-yard (12 m) line. Eli knew he had a chance to turn things around for his team and win the game.

Eli took the **snap**, dropped back three quick steps, and launched a perfect pass to **wide receiver** Plaxico Burress in the **end zone**. Touchdown! The Giants won 17–14.

Plaxico Burress was wide open in the end zone to catch Eli's pass.

Eli (#10) makes a pass while he's rushed by Patriots players.

To reach Super Bowl XLII (42), the Giants won three **playoff** games—all of them away games.

Super Bowl MVP

The Giants' victory in Super Bowl XLII (42) was a huge upset for the Patriots. New England entered the game with a perfect record—18 victories and no defeats. Most people thought the Patriots would win. Eli, however, had other ideas. He played hard to complete 19 out of 34 passes, including a key 32-yard (29 m) pass to David Tyree on the game-winning **drive**. During that play, Eli dodged several Patriots players, then hurled the ball far down the field. Leaping high, David Tyree made a spectacular catch by clutching the ball against his helmet. Because of Eli's incredible plays, he was named **MVP** of Super Bowl XLII (42).

David Tyree held the ball tightly as he was tackled by New England's Rodney Harrison (#37).

Eli held the Super Bowl trophy in the air alongside his coach, Tom Coughlin (right).

Eli was the second Manning in a row to earn the Super Bowl MVP award. The year before, Eli's older brother, Peyton, was named Super Bowl XLI (41) MVP.

All in the Family

Eli grew up surrounded by football. His dad, Archie Manning, was an **All-American** quarterback at the University of Mississippi, known as Ole Miss. Archie went on to play 14 seasons in the NFL.

Archie and his wife, Olivia, had three sons: Cooper, Peyton, and Elisha. Elisha "Eli" Manning was the youngest of the three boys. He was born on January 3, 1981 in New Orleans, Louisiana. As a child, Eli played football with the other kids in the neighborhood—and he was always the quarterback. Why? He could throw the ball better and farther than any kid his age.

Archie Manning played for the New Orleans Saints from 1971 to 1982.

Cooper and Peyton, Eli's brothers, were both star football players in high school. A medical condition ended Cooper's playing career, but Peyton went on to become a star NFL quarterback.

Archie (left), Eli (center), and Peyton Manning (right) are a family of quarterbacks.

His Father's Footsteps

When Eli reached high school, he became the **starting** quarterback for the varsity team. Eli had a great arm and always seemed to know what to do on every play. He earned the nickname "Easy" on the field. Why? Nothing seemed to bother him.

When it was time for Eli to pick a college, many schools wanted him to play for them. One of the colleges was the University of Tennessee, where Peyton had been a star player just a couple years earlier. However, Eli decided to follow in his dad's footsteps and attend Ole Miss. Eli went on to set or tie dozens of school records there. He passed for more yards and more touchdowns than any Ole Miss quarterback before him—or since.

As a high school student, Eli played football at Isidore Newman School in New Orleans.

The letter *C* on Eli's jersey showed that he was a captain of the Ole Miss Rebels.

Eli was not only a terrific quarterback at Ole Miss, he also worked hard in the classroom. He graduated from the school with a **degree** in marketing.

Fast Learner

After Eli graduated from college, he entered the 2004 NFL **draft**. The New York Giants wanted Eli to play for their team. Yet the San Diego Chargers got to pick first and chose Eli. So the Giants traded a player and three draft picks to San Diego in exchange for Eli. It was a big price to pay for any player, especially a quarterback who had yet to play in the NFL. However, the Giants have never regretted their decision. By the middle of his **rookie** season, Eli was playing like a champ and became the Giants' starting quarterback.

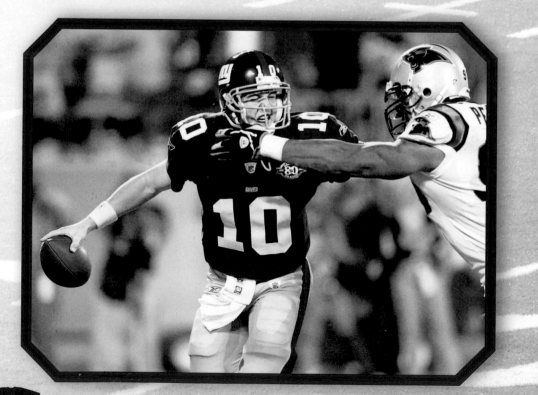

Eli is very good at moving quickly to avoid tackles.

Eli holds up a San Diego Chargers jersey, right before he was traded to the Giants.

Once Eli became a starter during the 2004 season, he has remained the starter for every Giants game for more than ten seasons.

Top of the Charts

Not everything went smoothly in Eli's rookie season. The Giants didn't have a very good team and lost many games. Although Eli attempted lots of great passes, many were **intercepted**.

In the last game of Eli's rookie season, though, he led his team to a big win. The Giants beat their biggest **rival**, the Dallas Cowboys. That was a sign of things to come. The next year, Eli passed for 3,762 yards (3,440 m) and 24 touchdowns. He also led the Giants to a **division** championship.

Four seasons after leading the Giants to a win over the Patriots in Super Bowl XLII (42), Eli did it again. He led his team in another game-winning drive late in the fourth quarter to beat New England 21–17 in Super Bowl XLVI (46)!

In 2014, Eli passed for more than 3,000 yards (2,743 m) for the tenth season in a row. No Giants player has passed for more career yards and touchdowns than Eli. He also made the **Pro Bowl** three times!

Eli became the Giants' all-time leader in passing yards during the 2013 season.

Helping Hands

Eli is much more than an incredible quarterback. He's also passionate about helping others. In August 2005, the most destructive hurricane ever to hit the United States landed in Louisiana. At least 1,600 people died during the storm, which was called Hurricane Katrina. Thousands of others were left homeless. Eli couldn't just sit by and watch as his hometown of New Orleans was destroyed. He had to do something to help.

Eli and Peyton **donated** money to help Katrina's victims. They also got in touch with the Red Cross. The relief organization told the brothers exactly what kinds of supplies were needed. That's when Eli and his brother rolled up their sleeves and filled boxes with water, diapers, pillows, and other items. They loaded the boxes on a plane headed to Louisiana.

The high winds and floodwaters of Hurricane Katrina destroyed thousands of houses, including this one.

Eli joined other volunteers in cleaning up the streets after Hurricane Katrina.

A year after Hurricane Katrina, Eli went back to Louisiana to help his dad, his brothers, and local coaches teach children about football. He wanted to help the children of New Orleans feel normal again after the hurricane.

For the Children

Eli also cares deeply about helping children. When Eli was still in college, he would sometimes visit sick kids at the Blair E. Batson Hospital for Children in Jackson, Mississippi. He knew a visit from a star quarterback could brighten a child's day. After he became an NFL quarterback, he decided to raise money to open a new clinic at the hospital. Beginning in 2007, Eli helped raise nearly $3 million. In 2009, the Eli Manning Children's Clinic opened. It treats more than 75,000 young patients each year! "There's great joy in knowing how many families and children you've helped," Eli says.

Eli and his wife, Abby, work together to help children at the Blair E. Batson Hospital.

Eli is always happy to sign autographs for his young fans.

Eli's **charity** work for kids is close to his heart. Why? He and Abby have three young daughters: Ava, Lucy, and Caroline.

Community

When the charity March of Dimes needed help in 2015, they called Eli. It was the seventh year in a row that Eli had helped with their biggest fundraiser of the year, the March for Babies. He joined more than 8,000 people to raise money to help improve the health of mothers and babies.

For many years, Eli has also hosted a charity golf tournament for Guiding Eyes for the Blind. The organization raises money to provide guide dogs for people with vision loss or for children with a condition called **autism**. "Every year," Eli says, "I listen to people tell their story about how they're able to accomplish so much more in their lives because of having guide dogs. That's been very rewarding for me." Eli's commitment to his team and to his community makes him a true football hero.

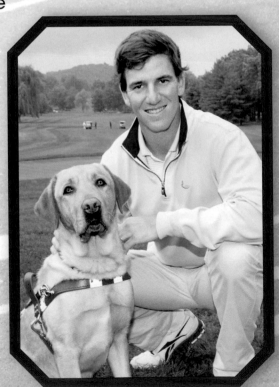

Eli was joined by a guide dog during the 2014 golf tournament he hosted.

Eli walks at a March of Dimes event.

In the Giants' win over the New England Patriots in Super Bowl XLVI (46), Eli was again named MVP. He is one of only five NFL players to win Super Bowl MVP honors more than once.

f dimes®

The Eli File

Eli is a football hero on and off the field. Here are some highlights.

🏈 Each year, the NFL's Walter Payton Man of the Year Award honors a player for his excellence on the field and community involvement off the field. Eli has been the Giants' nominee for the award four times.

🏈 Eli is at his best when a game is on the line. For example, of his 29 touchdown passes in the 2011 season, Eli threw 15 in the fourth quarter.

🏈 The Giants beat the San Francisco 49ers in the NFC Championship Game in the 2011 season. With that victory, Eli became the first NFL quarterback ever to win five playoff games on the road.

🏈 Eli remembers seeing the impact his father made and the joy he got from raising money to find a cure for the disease cystic fibrosis. This inspired Eli to devote himself to helping people in need.

Glossary

All-American (AWL-uh-MERR-ih-ken) a college player who is named one of the best at his position in the country

autism (AW-tiz-um) a condition that makes it hard to communicate or be with other people

charity (CHA-rih-tee) helping people in need

degree (di-GREE) a level of education completed

division (dih-VIZH-un) the way teams are grouped in a sports league

donated (DOH-nayt-uhd) gave something as a gift

draft (DRAFT) an event in which professional teams take turns choosing college athletes to play for them

drive (DRIVE) in football, a series of plays by the offense, usually ending in a scoring play

end zone (END ZOHN) the area at either end of a football field where touchdowns are scored

intercepted (in-tur-SEP-tuhd) passes that are caught by a player on the defensive team

MVP (EM-VEE-PEE) letters standing for *Most Valuable Player*

NFL (EN-EF-EL) letters standing for *National Football League*

playoff (PLAY-off) a post-season game played to determine a champion

Pro Bowl (PROH BOHL) the yearly all-star game for the season's best NFL players

rival (RYE-vul) a team that competes for the same goal

rookie (RUK-ee) a player in his first year in a league

snap (SNAP) the exchange of the ball from one player to another to begin each NFL play

starting (START-ing) playing at the start of a game; the best player at a position

wide receiver (WIDE ree-SEE-vur) a player whose job it is to catch passes

Bibliography

Cademartori, Lorraine. *"Eli Manning"* (from *"The Young and The Restless: The Top 20 Philanthropists Under 40"*). Observer.com (April 1, 2015).

Walton, Marsha. *"Manning Brothers Team Up for Katrina Relief."* CNN.com (September 5, 2005).

www.giants.com

Read More

Christopher, Matt. *On the Field With . . . Peyton and Eli Manning.* New York: Little Brown (2008).

Sandler, Michael. *Eli Manning and the New York Giants: Super Bowl XLVI (Super Bowl Superstars).* New York: Bearport (2013).

Scheff, Matt. *Eli Manning: Football Superstar (Superstar Athletes).* North Mankato, MN: Capstone (2014).

Learn More Online

To learn more about Eli Manning and the New York Giants, visit **www.bearportpublishing.com/FootballHeroes**

Index